So Often the Pitcher Goes to Water until It Breaks

# So Often the Pitcher Goes to Water until It Breaks

Poems by Rigoberto González

University of Illinois Press

Urbana and Chicago

© 1999 by Rigoberto González

Manufactured in the United States of America

P  5  4  3  2

⊚ This book is printed on acid-free paper.

Library of Congress Cataloging-in-Publication Data

González, Rigoberto.

So often the pitcher goes to water until it breaks :

poems / by Rigoberto González

p.   cm. — (National poetry series)

ISBN 0-252-06798-3 (paperback : perm paper)

1. Mexican Americans—Poetry. I. Title. II. Series.

PS3557.04695 S6 1999

811'.54—dc21

98-58019

CIP

# The National Poetry Series

The National Poetry Series was established in 1978 to ensure the publication of five poetry books annually through participating publishers. Publication is funded by James Michener, The Copernicus Society of America, Edward J. Piszek, The Lannan Foundation, and The Tiny Tiger Foundation.

## 1998 COMPETITION WINNERS

Rigoberto González, *So Often the Pitcher Goes to Water until It Breaks*
Selected by Ai, published by the University of Illinois Press

Harry Humes, *Ghost Pain*
Selected by Pattiann Rogers, published by Milkweed Editions

Joan Murray, *Looking for the Parade*
Selected by Robert Bly, published by W. W. Norton

Ed Roberson, *Atmosphere Conditions*
Selected by Nathaniel Mackey, published by Sun and Moon Press

Lee Ann Roripaugh, *Heart Mountain*
Selected by Ishmael Reed, published by Viking Penguin

For Texaco Alex, my truest friend

# Acknowledgments

*Americas Review:* "The Flight South of the Monarch Butterfly"; "Ghostory"; "Show and Tell: How My Grandmother Taught Me to Read Spanish"

*Borderlands: Texas Poetry Review:* "Marías, Old Indian Mothers"; "Penny Men"; "Perla at the Mexican Border Assembly Line of Dolls"; "You and the Tijuana Mule"

*Hayden's Ferry Review:* "Before the First Man Stepped on the Moon"

*James White Review:* "Body Maker"; "Taking Possession"

*El Locofoco:* "The Man Who Learned about Origami"

*Mockingbird:* "Day of the Dead"; "Mortician's Secrets"; "The Slaughterhouse"; "So Often the Pitcher Goes to Water until It Breaks"

*Morpo Review:* "The Exhibitionist Umbrella Salesman"; "What Smells Dead"

*Poet:* "Craft of the Candlestick Maker"

*Ruah:* "Response to the Sidewalk Preacher"

*Tall House Review:* "Abuelo Photographs"; "Stars Breaking"

"The Flight South of the Monarch Butterfly" and "Ghostory" also appear in *The Floating Borderlands: Twenty-Five Years of U.S. Hispanic Literature,* ed. Lauro Flores (Seattle: University of Washington Press, 1998).

"Marías, Old Indian Mothers," "Penny Men," "Perla at the Mexican Border Assembly Line of Dolls," and "You and the Tijuana Mule" also appear in *The Geography of Home: California and the Poetry of Place,* ed. Christopher Buckley (Berkeley: HeyDay Books, 1999).

A number of these poems also appear in the limited edition chapbooks *The Night Don Pedro Buried His Best Friend the Rooster,* ed. Gary Soto (Berkeley: Chicano Chapbook Series, 1998) and *Skins Preserve Us*, ed. C. G. Macdonald (Davis, Calif.: Agitator Dogs Press, 1999).

Thanks to Sandra McPherson, Maurya Simon, and Francisco X. Alarcón, mentors whose advice and insight are present in my work. Thanks also to my close friends for their patience, support, and sense of humor.

# Contents

So Often the Pitcher Goes to Water until It Breaks

# The Slaughterhouse

**1.**

Listen.
The slaughterhouse is empty
but you can still hear the squealing—
the echoes, people call them.
These can never leave; they are trapped
inside the walls like stains of blood.

Perhaps,
when the pigs heard their own cries,
they thought they didn't hear their own pain.
All sounds spin inside this house.
They confuse even the pigs.
Pigs don't know when to stop the noise.

**2.**

How strange
that the dogs come near enough
to sniff, but they won't eat the scraps.
They keep their distance, barking,
not at the swine, but at the men
who hang the carcasses on hooks

like coats.
A pyramid of pig heads
stares out the open door: outside

the men wash off their blood-gloves
in a trough bordered black with flies.
The dogs follow to lick their hands

but stop,
taking their liver-tongues back.
The men's hands still stink of knife blades,
of prongs, and of those fingers
that knot the rope so well. So many
smells. But no one smells the same pig.

3.
That's me
standing behind a dead sow.
I am tiny as its piglet.
My father took the picture
on my first visit to the house.
I remember it was taller

than church,
but narrow, like an alley.
The intestine strings in the back
didn't look like rosaries then;
they were intestines, running down
to meet the blood pool on the floor.

The sow
looks like she's fencing me off
to the wall, like she has swallowed
half my body. Or is it me
coming out of her pink belly,
born at the moment of her death?

4.

Listen.
The slaughterhouse is quiet now.
The gates have lifted to receive
one eyelid for every eye.
Darkness can be so maternal:
blood spots tip down like baby heads.

# The Flight South of the Monarch Butterfly

They always return to make us warm here in Michoacán
because they remind us of fire: they sputter like candles,
expanding and shrinking their singed browns and reds
as they consume the air in November, finally tapering down

into the shadows like burnt paper. What message
do they carry on their wings from the North—
the place that gave them a brush of black opal
for weight and touches of white to attract the clean

clouds and fool the sun into sending its brightest rays
through the mimic of holes? The butterflies settle their lit
bodies on the naked tree, bringing back its autumn leaves,
those breaths of orange that gasp before falling off again,

this time into the hands of winter. But here, winters
are warm like manzanilla tea. Haven't we always known that,
those of us who chose to stay within arm's length
of our mothers? But for some women, sitting like wooden saints

at their doors, these butterflies are calls for blessings
from their sons, the men whose names trickled down to thirst
inside their mothers' mouths. To them, the monarch's eggs
complete their prayers like rosary beads, they are the flammable

heads of matches. But we value the chrysalis of bone,
the blue shell that brings down the sky within our reach.

By March, when the monarch leaves, a second fever
strikes: the butterflies cluster into wreaths. The trees

the women's sons once owned are set ablaze again; young boys
raise their sticks to cut them down in flames.
We watch together as butterflies drop—explosions bright
as fireworks without sound, yet loud enough to call us out.

# Horn

By the road in Guerrero
a cattle cargo truck stops
at an incline with a flat.

Two brown bulls stand on the bed,
bound by the horns to a yoke—
each captive, hoof-bruised and skinned

at the talus, depending
on his partner for balance.
At the feet, a splash of blood

fiery as a spill of satin,
bubbling down like lava.
A wound burning through the wood?

Not so. The left bull's left horn
broke and flew off the head like
a bottle cap. Defected,

the horn dropped into the brush,
biting through, tip down, making
its first indentation on

its own. Now the bull's skull's left
unplugged like the puckered lip
on a plastic baby made

hollow by an absent thumb.
Stone Anahuac gods have mouths
that empty, that round. This hole's

center is sticky as if
the bull had stuck its black tongue
inside for comfort, the way

we tickle the missing tooth's
gum. Will it grow another?
The bull's left eye, panic-struck,

doubts it, set ablaze with pain.
The head's third socket shocks him
into thick paralysis.

The second bull doesn't move,
contemplating a collapse.
He gazes at his partner—

eye reflecting throbbing eye.
There is no seeking pity,
no screwing the horn back on.

# At the Panteón San Franciscano, Michoacán

Young boys skip out, rattling their coins
in plastic buckets. They take on their washcloths
the names of the dead, the death dates
and the snail trails of incomplete arcs.
Behind them, two old widows follow
locked at the elbows. They merge into a single
shadow; the wind blows one black skirt.
They greet the watchman at the gate,
both nodding their heads at one time.
The widows take with them their husbands' wilted wreaths
to fertilize the rose and the camelia.
The evening darkens the slabs
of cement; the graves look wet, fresh again.
On two tombs, green flower stems lean like tilted
candles in their pots while the watchman,
holding his hat to his head with one hand,
walks between them, outwhistling the wind.

# Day of the Dead

Before, it was a fascinating game
we played with our dead: a candy skull
wearing my abuelo's sugared name

across its front, a molasses-coffin full
of sweetened bones, a picnic on his grave
spread out on marble. Abuela, in her dull

black apron and rebozo (who saved
her best conversations for the tombstone)
said that joking with the dead will pave

a smoother, shorter path into their lone-
ly voyage. While women talked about the dying
and men toasted their tequila, I craved the bone

with its seven sweet letters winding
into my abuelo's name. I licked off the cursive *O*
and left the other six sticky with saliva, drying.

I would not remember that innocent theft
which transformed "Candido" into "Candid," until the day
I took my bottle to the tombs, bereft

of my own mother, her name written and displayed
on some ridiculous, purple-flowered head.
I could not reason anything to say,

thinking of that horrible truth spread
like honey, calling maggots to the dead.

# Plañidera: Professional Mourner for Hire

When her husband died, Merced held
back her best tears. He knew she would

and encouraged it, giving her few reasons in life
to cry. She stored them in her fingers—insurance, like

the crocheted creations behind
the bed, whose eyelets of yarn and thread she extended

only with the failure of the crops: six doilies bought
a week's nixtamal; a tablecloth kept even the chicken feet

fat. But the box behind the bed was emptied soon,
holding nothing but the needles, rattling like bones

too tough to grind. And she couldn't work anymore:
her eyes were tangled black yarn knots, her fingers

had stiffened into hooks, too outgrown to match
the meekness of a simple stitch,

too wide to round off a loop. She knelt at her
husband's grave, squeezing out the tiny reservoir

of tears: one knobby finger pressed against
the sharp socket of her eye unlocked her second start.

Here began her new career, a crying woman—
a plañidera—hired to aleluya and amén

for the rich man's final mass (sometimes
the only one who attends). The wealthy claim

devoutness in their end, providing posthumous
charity. And thus, the perfect compromise:

the women mourn a trail to the graveyard of the rich,
are paid their dues, and contribute to the church

one-tenth their wages. And this is what Merced
became—a llorona, sanctioned by the church's need

for the honesty of tears. She'll knit her hands
into her head, until her fingers unbend

to the half-tapered candle stubs the sexton
splits open to peel out the unburnt string, then

throws back into the boiling vat of wax.

# Walking by the Panteón San Franciscano

NOTICE

*Effective fifty years after the date of your death,*
*those of you who don't pay perpetuity will be uprooted.*
*For more information, please walk over*
*to the civil registry. Ask for Chela.*

In this cemetery, you can buy perpetuity
with pesos. For only fifty, you can keep
the mossy hair you'll never learn to comb,

the fingernails you'll forget to stick in your mouth
for comfort, though even if you remember,
your fingers will slip out just after the lips

slide in. You can have the shroud that will eat
through your skin after you've split the seams
on your sleeping shirt. But you will own every button

on that shirt and every bead on your rosary and every ring.
And though the beads and the stones won't wake anymore,
you can be sure they're safe, collecting at the bottom

of your coffin. And your teeth, oh yes, those teeth
in the back of your mouth, the ones you never used
or saw, even those will be finally yours to keep.

But you'll also keep more valuable things, like your cross,
yes, you can even keep your cross—
that gold-plated cross your godparent wrapped around

your catechism or the all-gold one your mother gave up
when you married in the church she and your father married in.
Whichever one you end up with, you'll keep.

Isn't that what you, a good Catholic, will want to do?
You'll crease each finger over the knuckles, both
knuckles over the chest, and then the ribs will cave in

over the lump of dust which used to be your heart.
And you'll fold over and over again until you are
layers of thin tissue, pious as a Bible.

Don't be fooled if your cross seems to have grown:
you have tried to shrink down to the size of your cross.
You have tried to be devout and hinge yourself on it

like a miniature Christ. And that will be
your own little secret blasphemy to keep in a box
and tuck away the way you used to store

old love letters, the way you will store your own tongue.
This you will learn and this knowledge too
you will keep. And no one will take that

or anything else away from you. No one
will ever search inside your pockets or disturb
the way you pile up your ash or tip your skull.

For only fifty pesos, you can keep all those things
you took with you—the few belongings even God
won't rattle in His collection plate.

# In the Week of the Dead, Masked

The jealousy stemmed from the mating habits
of rabbits. Although abundant, they kept
their numbers down during the rainy season,
thinning out like the rays of the sun. And like the sun
the business of rabbit meat went down.

But madroño and encino grew thicker
with the rain, strengthening the wood-crafts business.
When the hunter and the mask maker exchanged numbers
in the bar, the mask maker sold three faces
for each of the hunter's hares. Not long

after that, the craftsman was accused of dead-raising:
the rabbit hunter, who hid among the corn,
swore that his cousin, the mask maker, was dropping
corpse heads into a copper pot—heads with sharp
sockets like the rounded ends of a gun barrel.

The heads were ashen as stones, he said, each one
dismissing the captives of the eye
in one loud hiss as it sank
into its oil bath. The rabbit hunter swore he saw
each deathbed scene rise up into the sky—

feet, candles, Christs, old mothers on their knees,
all linked together by a string of smoke,
as in a rosary. And, yes, there were groans,

pleas too strong to keep each head from drowning,
too weak to force their way up under the cauldron's lid.

In the week of the dead, these events were common.
So the hunter vanished, taking his story back to the hills—
laughter chasing him off the way the rain sends
the mountain rodents back inside their lairs
of rock, stricken numb-cold in the dark.

Meanwhile, under thatched shade, the mask maker
chiseled and chipped, scooping out the inside
of a block of boiled wood, now dry and reduced to its rind
like a pumpkin shell. And on this shell
he ice-picked two holes for eyes, two for nostrils,

then he cut in the mouth, narrow as a knife slit.
He painted in the rabbit hunter's brows, next,
then his needle-thin whiskers, stitch-black.
He hung the mask in his hut, waiting for his cousin
to climb out of his hole and put his face back on.

# The Night Don Pedro Buried His Best Friend, the Rooster

He was on his way to bury his best friend, the rooster,
when la curandera stepped out of the smell of sage
and alcanfor
to ask for the tail feathers
that brush off all evil as easy as dust
that collects at the feet of saints,
or maybe, señor, don Pedro, if you would be so kind
as to let me have his comb
since he won't need to prick up the ends
like the tips of machete blades
the way the men used to jab them up in the old days
when they defended their honor
or impressed their wives-to-be,
not where he has gone, where all good roosters go,
to sing to the holy keeper of the holy gate—San Pedro,
don Pedro, and you know this machito
fathered enough black chickens to sweep
a hundred demons from the most attractive corners
of the souls of innocents, where
all of Satan's servants
strive to carve their sulfur caves;
but don Pedro didn't even want
to give up the rooster's right leg,
which could have been used to scrape off a curse
or two as they hovered above the front door
like wasps around their nest,

and in reality, my kind curanderita,
he has done his share of healing already,
didn't you say so yourself
that it was *my* rooster's wings
that blew the first breath into the Maldonado baby
the time doña Graciela brought him to your house
and the baby was the color of goat fat
crackling over an open fire, sweating like it too,
except the baby was cold as the first morning of winter
when even the watchman complains about his sleep,
and wasn't my rooster the only being that moved,
flapping his wings to remind the world to spin
after everybody else had let it stop,
all holding their breaths at once,
and how about the time my rooster
crowed at two in the morning . . .
and don Pedro would have gone on and on and
on like the crowing at two in the morning,
which begins in one beak
and continues in another, and in the end
even the beak that began doesn't remember
where it all got started,
but this rant began when
a curandera stopped don Pedro on his way
to bury his best friend, the rooster,
and bury him he did, between his father
and his father's second wife, who by the way,
my dear curanderita, was also a healer herself,
and that's when la curandera stepped back
and bowed her head,
in respect for the rooster
or for the stepmother the healer,
don Pedro wasn't sure,

all he wanted to be sure of that night
was that his best friend kept his feathers
the way any man kept his best suit, clean and pressed
for the final wear, so don Pedro wasn't surprised at all
when upon hearing one rooster crow,
then another, and another,
he could tell—sí, sí, sí, mi querida curandera—
could he tell the difference.

# Sentimental Undertakers

A peso was heavy once, you remember,
and big as the Eucharist, with Morelos
stamped on top—Morelos puckered and kissable.

He kept quiet in your fingers
as you snuck him past your mother
though he was meant to stay in church on Sunday mornings.

When Morelos bought you crackers with chipotle sauce
you weren't too sad to give him up—he always came back.
But then Morelos wouldn't return

as frequently: you rarely saw him on the bus,
fat-cheeked and stoic beneath his paisley
headwrap; the schoolgrounds slowly missed

his mediating games of marbles or his launching
Moctezuma coins in a round of cuartas.
Even the garbanzo lady wouldn't take him

anymore, fanning the brasero and holding out
for the monk-frock color of a ten-peso bill.
Your commitment to the coins

had ended, you would have us think.
But Celio, the little Celio of the front seat
of the hearse, who napped inside a coffin once,

scolded by your father for having picked
the wrong size, you've been
hiding pesos in a locked tin box under your bed.

Your mother asked you why
you collected stones. Stones? You kept that
from her too, the way you keep

the clipped fingernails of the dead, but those
only long enough to try on. You're as sentimental
as your father, also a Celio, and you're

learning as he once did, to send an invocation
with the just-deceased.
Your grandfather, another Celio, gave each fist

a cherry pit so that heavens could bloom
the way hillsides on Michoacán did not;
so that heavens would receive him in red.

Your father slides a broken butterfly into one
pocket. When the cemeteries come alive again,
so will the winds, bursting into oranges

and yellows, colors those winds now hesitate
to carry. And you, the smallest Celio, will bring
into our afterlife our small change

childhood of centavo loterías
and colaciones, of a México before the single
peso, single pleasure, disappeared.

## Doña María Greets Her Comadre Doña Luna at the Balcony Window

So you're staying up again, doña Luna, waiting
to guide my sons home from the bar.
Then let me help you push out the dark with this face
these hands have wrinkled, a face shaped
the way a restless woman shapes
the folds and furrows on the sheets. How do you
manage it, señora? How do you keep your fingers
from digging into those worries half-stitched

against eyelids? What stops you from throwing down
your cheeks like bowls of beans gone bad, waiting
for the spoon that never comes? What thoughts
swirling within you don't break you off and chisel you?
Someday I too will be bald as rock, having unspooled
the last thread from my head. There is no shame in that.
It's what makes us comadres, a pair of copper cazuelas,
identical molcajetes from the mother stone—

the stone that knows how to hold its breath; the stone
that watches and teaches how to watch; the stone
that keeps the earth in its proper place; the stone
that separates the oceans from the skies; the stone
that stops the floods and snuffs out fires;
that lid of stone, which seals our deaths.
And this old woman will have her peace when her tongue
shatters and all her complaints dissolve into ash.

But you are the unlucky one, aren't you, doña Luna?
Because you will open your eyes a thousand nights
after God has pressed His thumb over my heart
and that night will be the same as the nights before.
And you'll see how one thousand nights after that,
worriers and insomniacs still call on you, supplier
of the knitting needle, rocker of the cradle, guardian
of the blue mazorca, keeper of the restless fish.

How everyone looks up to you as if you could solve
the riddles in our dreams, as if you had risen
solely to cut through the darkness of our sleep.
How many times we will expect you to tame bad dreams:
when the child awakens suddenly, with a glint of light
scaring his eye, you'll be asked to help him see within you
the harmless white in a dead hen's tongue,
the Lord's round ear, the hand that received his birth.

And this boy will become a man, and that man
might awaken one night to that familiar boyhood fear
and you will soothe him then too, showing him his bride,
her breast, her belly, the wheel that spins inside.
And this man will become an old man, having long since
learned to identify in you his tempered wisdom,
which he will always believe he achieved on his own,
which will trick him into climbing through that hole

and into the pit of the other side.
And another man will rise from the dust,
and another man will unhook his hands from his jaw
to let his voice fly home. And still
nothing puts you out of your sky, nothing—

not the girls who grow their hair beneath you, collecting
secrets like combs and letting in dusks like bedmates;
not the women who round off their faces beneath you,

taking your lines to their calves, your color to their heads;
not the old women who beneath you weave their own shrouds
night after night after night. And every night
is the same night. You were given no choice;
all this time you could have faced the other way
or maybe all this time you never looked our way
and kept us ignorant, because it never mattered that we named
the back of your head "el farol de enamorados,"

expecting you to open a mouth and bring out that passion
called tongue; to lift up the nose like a skirt—
such sweet smells; to expand the cups of the hands,
the pillows of the thighs; to part every cleavage and limb
and expose the hidden moistures caught between dark
and light. How much does it matter if you ever tried
to show us different, when we'll always believe
it is you sending lust through our veins? You're to blame

though when we jerk our heads like owls, trapped in the woods
by the noises of night, you give us your quilt
and say nothing. When we show you the sores on our feet,
those tears on our skins like old clothes,
you give us stitches and expect nothing.
So what comes next? Do we lift our empty hands and mouths
in your direction, and will you, kind señora, kind
mother, take nothing in exchange for your bread?
Poor doña Luna, poor comadre, there is no rest for you.

We have given you so much responsibility, we've forgotten
what tiny bones we have, what small spaces we occupy.
Today, here we are: comadres, a pair of curandera eggs
sucking up the cries that keep the alleys wide.
Tomorrow, my body may adjust itself under the sheets
and you'll wait up for other sons alone, señora. That's why
I'm here now, weak and sleepless, pretending this night
I'll pluck one burden off your eye.

# Catarina's Dress Rehearsal

First time at a portrait studio—
the new photographer's invitation: SEEKING
SAMPLES FOR THE WINDOW. Catarina, you're so india
pretty, so photogenic in those high tarasco cheeks. Catarina:

age twelve, gap-toothed, and without a pair of shoes,
but with a sister who can weave a ribbon
into a crown of eyelets and lace like on a Mexican actress
of black and white matinees, a woman whose suitor's

mustache opens a ditch on the movie screen
each time he smiles, sings.
Catarina, men respect the art of a temple curl's inverted
question mark and won't unpunctuate its grace.

Catarina shakes the cracker crumbs off
the lime dress with the collar crawling up the throat
in Catholic schoolgirl fashion.
The torn hem above the knee won't show.

The photographer can hide
the mango stain with shadows, just like in cinema shots—
imperfections all secrecy, all discretion.
Neighbor, may we borrow the centerpiece

of silk flowers in the  vase that sparkles
like the bottle of a movie queen's perfume? The neighbor
offers her daughter's sock-scented shoes as well,
if Catarina wears them only for the picture.

She had never worn shoes; Catarina
gives each one to the wrong foot. The toes
point out, poised to run from her body.
Even better, thinks the photo-man,

whose flash of light pierces straight through the wall.
Catarina, an immortal on film, two-
dimensional as María Félix enraged, as a weeping
Libertad Lamarque. Blinded, Catarina breaks up into sound

like a Dolores del Río exclamation forced off
the screen, out of the movie house, into the street.
The marquee grows dark, and Catarina's voice
keeps ringing stars when the velvet curtains close.

# The Exhibitionist Umbrella Salesman

The butcher's wife who lived across the street
preserved no details of him. Like us,
she couldn't undo what she had learned:
confuse the ribs and muscles on his belly
with the edges of the windowpane;
merge his navel, the chaos of his body hair
with chrysanthemum shadows creeping off the ledge.
If he had ever spoken, she never listened:
to admit he had a voice would grant him
a quickness responding to light, a provocation
that would only inch him forward.
When asked about those mornings
sitting at her Singer, when the curtains opened
on the second floor of doña Guille's boardinghouse,
the buther's wife recalled the houseplants on the ledge
and the rumor of some salesman
who came to town about the time the drought did.
A solicitor, he was meant to be avoided,
rejected, but in discreet and Catholic manner.
We didn't need them, but we purchased his umbrellas,
one bat's wing at a time. We kept them shut
to deprive him of the space to shake them open.
We kept them shut, thinking he'd leave our town
much sooner and that just as quickly we'd forget him
naked at the window, dripping from the heat
beneath his black umbrella, or so the whispers,

which was enough. We saw too much of him walking down the street,
teasing us with his umbrella sack,
fingering the cords at the end of the umbrella shaft.
Those who couldn't avoid doña Guille's street
would confront him with his product,
compensating the impoliteness of not looking up to wave
by tilting the umbrella forward, just a bit.
And when the salesman left, we weren't sure
if he was running from the rain or the rain from him
or even if they traveled the same direction.
We welcomed the clouds
but never agreed if the man at doña Guille's
and the salesman were indeed the same man
or if there had been a man at all.
The butcher's wife remembered only the houseplants.
Yet the schoolboys kept alive the joke about some man
and his umbrella, which matured inside the local bar,
still only a joke, and not an image any man admitted
to having seen.
Despite all that we still own black umbrellas,
which we haven't opened. Warns the superstition:
never use ten years after a drought.

# Craft of the Candlestick Maker

Wood chips scattered like moth wings on the floor
will prove how time can materialize
its minutes. This is a pile of hours
the candlestick maker shaved with a blade.
And this is the man whose hand guides
the knife through the wood's thick skin.

With each slow stroke, his thumb restores
its callus, which hardens like a slice
of candle fat. He presses down to rub off scars
and flatten nubs until a rib-thin stick remains—
a bone, its new guise tough-veined, erect with pride,
but lonely, holding up its only socket or pin,

that spike for impaling a tallow wife. It's more
like a sacrifice than a candle playing bride
in that frigid room, among the saints so dour
in their dusty robes, the candle-Christs raining
impassioned beads of sweat down their sides.
The stick is also a stake at which to burn the sins

of dead Catholics—their funerals melt only four
at a time. There, litanies turn to smoke and rise
because the candlesticks were made upright, made to devour
candles like witches at the fire until the shades
of mourners tire of watching and wither to their corners
when the mouth-holes bite down. The mysteries spin

inside the stick's cup, grail-shaped, blessed before
its service. The maker works by candlelight,
polishing the wood with wax, matching the luster
on his skin—a piety that tames the candle flames,
keeping them from eating up the silk, those white
clean slips the Virgins raise over the paraffin.

# Before the First Man Stepped on the Moon

On the seventh day
when the seas drew back
and the salt in the pools the seas
left behind had time to seep
into the land, becoming sweet,
the Lord wiped His right hand
and the dust dropped down
on the lakes of Michoacán
to soak up the surface
and bloom into lilies
whose petals smell like the bellies
of the fish.

The truth was
the fish learned
how to smell like lilies, and from them
learned how to rub off their scales
on the sides of the lava stone;
how to stretch their mouths
to suck in the sun; how to gather like petals
and how to disperse,
not with touch but with sound.
And it was there, before the fisherman knew
how to knit a net or unwind a line,
that these fish learned

how to walk on water.
At first it was a sleepwalk, a nightly
balance on the tailfin—a float
over the surface like the unsettled hands
of the drowned reaching up
or like the reflections
of stars not quite settled down,
and it was no miracle.
Nor was this walking forced on them
by the lilies who pushed themselves
closer to shore to make room.
The fish flipped open their gills

and let the moon slip down
their sides and expand underneath them
as if its reflection helped them remain
afloat. So when the first man pushed
a crooked canoe to the center of the lake,
he could not keep from plucking
those wet buoys, those beautiful
fleshed-out lilies as healthy and edible
as the mammal hearts and lungs
he loved to suck dry.
The story of the lilies continues:
they had taught the fish

to tempt our hands
to lift them to our teeth.
From that night on, the fish
were to take their deaths
in their mouths to dissolve inside ours.
So important they became we set

a space for them on our plates of clay,
decorated with lilies.
And the lilies took back the lake
unnoticed, incidentally
as the hand
that first dropped them there.

Let it be told, then,
that the fish willed to remain
underwater.
Let it not be confused
with the tragic tale of the snake who
also knew how to walk and who
gambled away that power *and* the ability to speak
when it shared the garden.
The fish knew how to walk
long before any of them; long before
the necessity of safety,
before the necessity

of boats, before the Ark
became necessary; before
man learned to pry open the mouths of fish
and remove gold; before
he learned to multiply fish
as quickly as crumbs from bread; before
he learned how pulling up the nets
to the Lord will unroot
the fish from the lake. Let us not forget
the necessity of fish
or the lessons of the lilies, because
after all that

when the first man took
the first step on the surface of the water,
stepping on the faint reflection of the moon,
if he had only looked back to the lakes
of Michoacán, he would have seen
he was still only imitating fish imitating lilies.

# Response to the Sidewalk Preacher

We've heard it all before: that the earth
will fold its arms into a knot
and squeeze out our cries with confessions; that the sea
will suck its saliva back in,
mimicking the thirsty mouths of the dead; that the sky
will put out its flame in one breath
and we'll prick our eyes shut in the dark;
that we'll take off our souls, those dirty shirts,
and our hearts will crack like hot glass in the cold.
All this tomorrow. Over and over, tomorrow.

Well, why not today? Already
the moon hovers like the inner curve of an empty bowl; already
the sun burns a hole through our tongues; already
the streets, those malpractice surgeons, cut us to halves
with their needles and knives and stand at the corner
to buy a cup of our diluted blood; already
a death certificate is a welfare check; already
we value sleeping pills like teeth; already
we wear our skins like potato sacks
and keep fingers in our pockets like tarnished spoons.

Give me that book in your hand. I'll eat it
like a sandwich; I'll sleep on it
like a mother's lap and empty my ear of bad dreams;
I'll hold it up to bandage the sky; I'll throw it

into the air and let it drop its faith like rain; I'll wear it
like a hat and tip it like a cornucopia.
If it's true what you say, preacher, that this book
holds the answers between its ribs, let me have it.
I'll chew through the bone, I'll get to the center,
I'll swallow it, I'll crush it like a third lung.

# Marías, Old Indian Mothers

Las Marías, our Indian mothers, have
disappeared. At the U.S.-México border, they used to walk
between our cars, with one child
attached to the ends of their braids
and four others peeling off
from their skirts like patches, like over-bellied pockets.

They used to hold up plastic cups for our coins,
closing their eyes with each thank you, offering
blessings too weak to take home.
Where did these women come from,
whose child-lumped backs trail off
into our rearview mirrors like ghosts or visions

from some long-ago vacation?
Are they from a hidden Mexican village
only the *National Geographic* could find?
Then how did they get here? Are they
husbandless or are they married to that pair
of sandals too tight to let them walk far, too large

to fit back into the narrow pathways
of uncharted towns? Have they slept under newspaper
headlines to produce such sorry-eyed children
that yawn away each minute, meatless as
a bone? When the children are old enough,
they'll learn to stretch their toes

into their mothers' footprints, each foot
cross-flat and empty as their supper plate.
Some of these children will wander
out of the lines and get lost, searching
for their missing mothers. Some of them
will lag behind, checking under vehicles

and inside policemen's boots, attempting
to detect the echo of the plastic cups.
People say the women found the same wind
that flew them here; the children were too heavy-eyed
to fly. Others say that the foreigners took them
and stuffed them and dust them weekly

at city museums. And some say the women simply
died, leaving nothing to the streets
except the smell of copper and the sound
of an arm coming down. But you and I know
they are indestructible, built to last
at least a century or two, rattling our coins

like pits, tolling our lucky
appetites. You and I know they are
where we last left them, waiting for us
to sew our hands back onto their skirts.
These Indian women have never gone
beyond our reach; it is we who have kept our arms

inside our cars and driven off
through that gate that divides us in half,
where we exchange our names, our eyes.
Now no one calls to us to look
back. Here, there is no one to lose—
there's no reason left to believe we have mothers.

# You and the Tijuana Mule

They're the dead ends
at this avenue's corners,
turning away the traffic
of tourists. They amuse only once
like a fire hydrant in green
or an inside-out calf at the butcher's.

But this joke is more perverse:
the light pole painter's solution
to an excess of thick black, cream,
and olive: stripes on mules—zebras!
Static as carousel horses
off the platform, they're heavier

at the belly, gravity
finally keeping their viscera
down; the rhythm of their head-shaking
is erratic, it's the wild hair
at the tail-tips. Each mule is irreplicable
in a coat of hand-painted stripes.

Take a second look. Next
to each mule stands a man.
Ignore his camera, forget about his
FIVE DOLLARS FOR A PICTURE.
Focus instead on his outline—
one-dimensional as a figure in chalk,

an upright paper cutout.
Work your way outward to the fumes
melting the blue in the sky,
to the exhaust pipes and the glare
of cracked windshields, to the mule
taking away the eye from the dull

colors on the building behind it
and from the light pole in front.
If you follow further to the left,
you'll reach another mule.
Further on you'll find an entire pack
of cars, filtering out the gate

and across the border at donkey
speed. But you don't need to go
that far to consider this: this corner
is a vanishing point, the absence
of the man leaves a hole sucking up
concrete, flesh and air, like a drain.

And you are avoiding it,
scurrying off as far north as you can, turning
only to see how far you've gotten.
Put the man back in like a plug.
Let him stop the pull, sinking in
like a drenched rag in the mouth

of a gas tank. In one hundred degrees of heat,
let him be more threatening. Pay him
five dollars, take your picture next to
(or on) the mule. Place yourself
within the man's breathing space and wonder
why you shudder in the middle of June.

# Perla at the Mexican Border Assembly Line of Dolls

Her job was to sort through the eyes
of dolls. Snapping hollow limbs
into plastic torsos had been a soothing task
for Perla, like arranging the peas back into the pod

or picking up spilled grains of salt, one by one.
Since she was born without a womb
and her ears closed up because no infant's shrill
had kept them open, Perla's fingers had developed

sensitivities to dolls: she exchanged
her gentle touch for their rigidity,
which stiffened her bones to the wrists;
at rest, her hands shut down like clamps.

But she could not refuse this trade.
Sometimes she became too easily attached
to the hands, whose curvatures embraced
the crooked joint of her index finger.

She'd go home with her pocket full of arms
too often and would bury them in her garden
in pairs: a right arm with a right arm,
a left one with a left—the fingers always pointing

down like roots. After seasons, the only growth
was the ache inside her bones, while her arms
kept shrinking, narrowing like stalks.
Perla asked to be moved to heads.

Here she was appalled by how strands of hair
are jabbed in with pink hooks, how noses and ears
are pinched out, and with what brute force
the mouth hole is ice-picked through.

And for years she had equipped these dolls
with arms too short to massage themselves.
Sometimes she had sent them off
without arms at all, and she imagined

the limbs in her garden digging deeper
into earth, like split worms madly searching
to comfort their severed halves.
So Perla requested the task of sorting eyes,

eyes that sink into her thumbs
the way rosary beads cave in fingerprints.
Yet here she doesn't count or pray;
she only teaches how to dull the pain.

Her gift with a squeeze of her rigid fingers
is the luster of the callused tips,
their stoic gaze. The dolls give up
the sensibility in eyes that do not blink.

The eyes freeze over like the surfaces
of lakes, while Perla's fingers feel again,
though everything she touches slices
clean into her most afflicting nerves.

With the pupil locked in place as if in ice,
each eye stares up accusingly at Perla
as she's about to push it into place: a tack
threatening to thrust back the fury of its nail.

# Penny Men

for Emiliano, who came to live, and die, picking grapes

These are the men from México's boot, the ones
who fell out from a hole in its bottom. They are bony
but well-attached as scissors. When they become
hungrier, they will cut their own stomachs
in half. They come to live like loose change

in a country that drops its pennies
and leaves them there; in a country whose jingle
of coins muffles the sound of backbones cracking.
These men squeezed through the gate, that slot,
and found the backroads with crosses

on which the grapevines wave their leaves
like dollar bills. Green, edible, the vineyards
promise to feed—to stuff—their pockets
though the cups of wine aren't theirs
to drink. Thirst concerns the boss no more than heat

or how much of it garlands each head.
After work, their faces glow sun-flat; they resemble
copper centenarios with dust instead of a bridge
over the nose, with a rust-heavy hinge for a mouth.
These faces promise to reveal exotic lands

and languages. But the bridges are impassable,
distant as the waters of a river on a map,
and the tongues are too tired to speak.

They sit beneath the pines for shade,
their heat-suffused hair steaming off. Precipitations

of sweat clean off their arms, those thin pokers
that stir the ash all day. They express no
criticism here, no shame. Their ears build up dirt
into stones inside their wells, at times confusing
the memory of a woman who speaks inside their sleep.

To stretch out the afternoon breeze, they play
blackjack and twenty-one, gambling bottle caps
instead of silver. Slowly, the darkness in their eyes
blends with the shadows; the sparkle of the caps
and beer can tabs ascends into the canopy of sky.

Beds are too luxurious; backseats too cramped
and sticky in summer. Some men prefer cool car hoods,
their own hands for pillows, the privacy of twilight.
The moon, their second mother, knits their sleeping
coats, which always fade away with stars.

Some dawns, not all the men wake up so quickly.
One man might sink too deep in dreams, clinging
to the woman he wishes he had never left—the woman
who throws her voice toward the North, whose words
stir up a breeze for all the men below.

# Death of the Farm Workers' Cat

Locked up until next season's harvest,
the communal shack holds in its final draft.

Rolled-up mattresses lie stacked awkward as
spiral shells with the hollows squeezed shut. A forgotten

cigarette stays cramped inside the crack of a wall,
numb as a flower bud. And because it was her habit, the black

cat crouches on the windowsill, white whiskers twitching,
waiting for the double doors to split.

The men will recognize the carcass—
the animal that crawled between discarded boots to

stiffen like a muddy sock. *Negra,* one man
called her. Another, *Sombra.* Yet another named her

*Cascabel,* what his sweetheart called her cat in Tuxtla.
Mumuring that name reminded him of murmuring

inside his lover's ear, of the indiscreet meows
that made his lover whisper *ssshhh!* half

alarm, half pleasure. In the shack, purrings
fluttered, delicate as lullabys. Fur

charged the heart through an electrostatic touch.
The cat seeks out that touch, shifting day and night

from wooden sill to concrete floor. At once patient,
leaning on the boots with the memory of feet, at once

restless, trapped behind the window with
her wet nose drying up against the glass.

# After Jaime the Refrigerator Man Shot Himself We Said

It must have started with his humming.
Crouched down behind the motors, he had practiced
imitating the imperfect rhythms—skipping beats
sporadically; strengthening and weakening vibrations
at unpredictable intervals; holding
his breath alongside the refrigerators
when he unplugged their cords, then catching up
to the fans' rotations when he plugged them in again.

He approached each refrigerator with its own cacophony,
courting it, taming it, making it easier to fix.
And lost in this complexity of soiled wires and coils,
he'd suddenly look up at us as if we'd caught him working
toward some forbidden pleasure. But only he
would know the rewards of fondling that intricate
body of warm metals and rubber tubes with curves
that wound around his arms. He'd hum continually,

matching the heat of the motor with his own
sweat, until the machine ran perfectly again.
But then Jaime left to explore the depths in motors
on the other side, leaving us our strange refrigerators
that wouldn't respond to the touch of any other man.
It was said that in the foreign land machines spoke
other tongues. We imagined Jaime's screwdrivers and wrenches
getting colder, shrinking down to the size of nails.

We imagined Jaime without his wife, no longer able
to press her hands against his throat
while he made love to her and she repeated the sounds
that she had learned from him. And maybe one night he flung
open the bedroom window to cool off his longing
for the sounds in México, but México shut down completely
the way the foreign land blacked out to silence
the second Jaime fit the gun's tip in his ear to listen.

# Rosario's Graveyard Shift at JFK Memorial Hospital

At 2:00 A.M. the light in the hallways sticks
to the walls. The fluorescence swallows
her uniform and she marches undetected,
her face peering out of a clipboard, white as her nurse's cap.

She is safe in her camouflage, having to walk
from wing to wing unarmed, without a needle
or a bottle of tablets rattling in her hand. She's
bold when she glances to the sides at this hour,

and for one quick look she is unashamed
to think: whose abuelos are these, these gauze-
haired mannequins who stoop each morning over
a clutter of plastic utensils, a bedpan, and a cup

or a bowl of green Jell-o? Metal bars surround
their oversized cribs. Do they mind their wrists
handcuffed to a small machine that counts
up or counts down to some booked destination? They cough

and wheeze, using up their words like pills. Yet even
when they speak they are too tired to call, these old
dolls that prop themselves up to unstick their lids,
each time leaning back to blink. Only Rosario's ear,

whisper-sensitive and paper cup clean, can admit to hearing
them manage a whimper or a groan. Even then she's quite
invisible rubbing their pale skins with oil
while they turn to the door and visitors gawk like birds

in their flowered shirts and dresses. What
do the passersby see that they won't find
in any other room with Rosario in it? Blank-eyed people
see only a sickness with weak limbs, see only

whiteness. Rosario, brown-faced, dissolves away
unnoticed, frequently ignored. Here, Rosario
is only part of the curtain. During linen changes,
she is only an extension of the sheets. Will Rosario

reach some compromise with the patients, at that point
when they open their eyes, glassy as if to offer her
a drop of water, and when her arm unfolds to find
the pitcher? Or when they attempt a smile

in the morning, a row of imperfect teeth
that pretend to possess a rind of light,
and when she smiles back, accepting their humble
gift, letting them think they own something?

There must be a middle ground where they can meet,
naked of these four-cornered cloths and pillows
designed to muffle cries at night. A place
where stitches can pass for wrinkles, scars

for stretchmarks, and where body parts are nailed
back on without the concern of matching color
or proportion, without that ceremony that ends
with short-lived roses and balloons that deflate

overnight. At 2:25 the nurse's light goes on
in room 308. Rosario pulls out a surgical mask
from her pocket and fades out of one dimension,
only to reappear discreetly in the next.

# Body Maker

My business, said the window dresser,
is body parts:
I button a blouse
and create breasts,
I bring up a zipper and give you a crotch.

Magic is
producing a neck
with a string of plastic
pearls or a scarf with dots.
Hand me a leather belt

and I'll make you hips that can bear
no children, but which can easily withstand
the weight of denim
all hours of the week. You haven't seen
a thigh until you've seen me

stretch the delicate hem
of a red skirt, just so,
midway to the knee.
My business is arms:
the less sleeve I use, the more skin.

Revealing a wrist
is safe enough, an elbow
is somewhat daring, calling attention
to its absence of wrinkles.
But let me fold back the entire sleeve and . . .

there you have it!
a shoulder, boldly upraised
to expose its mound under the light.
Tell me, where else have you seen
such perfection?

It took me
years of practice to get it right.
The mannequins out of the box
often lacked a finger or a foot,
and I returned them

to their wholeness by picking out
the right shade of black
in a suede boot or evening glove.
But sometimes not even a trenchcoat
could conceal the asymmetry

of a mannequin with a caved-in torso
as if its plastered heart
had been plucked out.
Those mannequins, those model
freaks keep me company in the storage room,

their arms down, defeated,
their faces pale, unmasked,
collecting dust like burnt-out bulbs.
We form our own community
of nudes, acquainting ourselves

with our true bodies when we
set free our bellies,
unhinge our backs,
unbuckle our feet,
and remove our hands.

# The Man Who Learned about Origami

Her face crimped into crêpe paper
when she died.
When her cheeks began to pleat,
her husband nodded in approval
though he wasn't Japanese.

No one had taught him
how to recognize art, yet there he stood
watching the corners of her lips
tuck themselves in for the night,
which was all nights folded into one.

Her eyes were the creases
he'd always known to stir at twilight, lids
slightly opened like baked clams.
That craft had reached its end;
he respected that.

The strain of keeping
each room its room,
the kitchen a kitchen,
and order in their shades of green and blue
was finally put to rest.

Images unloosened,
settled back in her skull,
urging her mouth ajar.

Though her upper lip cracked
like a paper moth under a heavy starch,

her husband still saw
the beauty of it all,
despite the wings' threat
to fall off before first flight.
She'll remain intact, he thought,

the crust will not drop
into the craters of the nose.
There are no heat-attracting smells
left, only memories of recipes
bound and flat on the page of her skin,

soon to fade like ink.
Her chin and forehead were but mountain folds
with ridges of reflected light—
no valleys, only one more gush
of grooves. Yet he learned

to value her
collapse of wrinkles, their confusions,
knowing his sharp features
were also corners, also softening,
also caving in on him.

# Widower

The table has been cut
in half. You sit alone,
your soup bowl a seashell.
You fill it up, spoon-stir
the passions of her breath.
But heat will not reveal
her secrets in that stew
that make your skin reject
your shirt. She left behind
no map to find that kiss
you carry on your back.

At night, the moths grow large,
snuff the light bulbs off.
The wind sneaks in to sweep
all whispers out. No yes,
no no, the bed will make
no noise. And you'll wake up
to think it was a dream
sweat-twisted in the sheets,
your hand deceived once more
by two warm mattress prints—
your heat on both bedsides.

# Mortician's Secrets

### 1.

The most righteous part of the body
is the armpit with its delicate growth of hair.
The armpit has withheld more gossip. It has kept quiet
more than our privates, complacent
in a corner that when exposed we choose to ignore.
That's how it became so respected:
it took advantage of our faces turned sideways, our embarrassed
looks, and then imitated that humility.

### 2.

Mouths always spit out their final sentences.
Until then the jaws remain locked as if biting down
on that last word: the location of the car keys, a cry
for help, the name of the face the dying recognized and thought
they could pronounce before closing shut. The dead
sometimes do this purposely—an attempt
at grasping the world they feared to leave behind; at holding
on to a memento, which could comfort them when pressed
slightly against the tongue. Sometimes it is
accidental that the word is there at all, having been
abandoned or compressed within the throat at the moment
of death. Either way, the mouth eventually lets go.
That word turned solid as a marble or a broken tooth
surrenders to the quietest of hours.

The word squeezes through the lips and reclaims
its ascension back to sound when it bounces
off the chin: a bead of sweat melting on the griddle—
a blue kiss coming up for air.

3.

A woman's ash tastes
different from a man's. Remember how as children
we shook the sawdust of old church floorboards
with our weight? While on our knees we
reached down to draw obscene figures, then licked
our fingers clean. A man's ash will remind us
of the days we mixed those pictures with the Host;
of catechism days when we spread the orange
coating of bricks to affect a bloody tongue
during silent prayer. A man's ash tastes of old *pinole,* of common
dust—bedroom dust sucked in excitedly
within the fury of sheets.

But a woman's ash is not as easily
compared. I can't explain it with anything
I've tasted, but certainly with elements I never dared
to touch. Taking her ash was like
discovering the outlines of the woman's fingers in the glove,
of the head beneath the hair. It was finally knowing
the taste of sugarcane pulp a woman discreetly
spits inside her napkin. It was digging out the thin
crust of dirt between her toes and around the curve of her heel.
It is something not quite forbidden or
inaccessible. It is the flavor of what could have been
and which I savor even more because it wasn't.

4.

Before the bodies leave the parlor, I dress them
in my coat. Not my black mortician's coat with its heavy
scent of lily stems and tarnish, but my blue one, the one
I haven't worn myself. It's not a body in my coat
that excites me, but rather that of my
fleshed-out coat inside a coffin,
its collar and shoulders pushed out against the lining as if
with the weight of the coat's deep color and not of
the corpse. In my coat the body vanishes. The face becomes
an afterimage. The gold buttons show through
the crossed hands. I'm persuading my burial coat
to be selfish, to want its own space, to keep itself company.
I'm teaching it to be its own body,
and like the body insist on reshaping the edges
of the coat on its own and on demanding
to twist and bend all objects in the parlor
toward itself. Already the lapel rejects
flowers whose petals don't fade
into blue. When I die I will dress my death in that coat
and allow my absence to become the main attraction.

# Show and Tell:
# How My Grandmother Taught Me to Read Spanish

The Mexican tabloids spell death
in capitals, always in red ink:
MUERTE, MUERTE. The *M*s' legs
are as thin as chicken bones;
their shoulders aim like cleavers.

Each week you spread out this paper
like a cookbook in the kitchen.
You drop a bowl in the sink,
splashing the front page with water, swelling
the headlines with goosebumps,

yet I can still read how this woman
kills her husband
by splitting his head in two. And you,
Abuela, can still stir the stew. See
the husband's skull divided

like a melon? Autopsied, he has stitches
thick as rope weaving up and up
through the middle of his ribs
like those television oven turkeys
that look too bright to eat.

It's the season of husbands, the caption
declares. There is the ax looking inoffensive
as a serving ladle, tucked gently

as a napkin between the woman's hands.
The woman smiles with the left side of her lip.

On page ten there's a child who falls
out of his sleep and onto the sidewalk
two stories down, only to have this sheet of letters
make his crib. Here is his photograph in black
and white: it's a tiny dumpling, Abuela,

his blood is the color
of soy. See the babysitter? Her hands
reach out of her photograph as if that were
the window that had helped the infant out.
See the sad people? See the dead

people? People with distant names
as far as the hills of México.
On page twenty there are plenty
of faces looking down at their obituaries,
wearing their names on their toes.

And here, Abuela, is your name
in print. What it would look like if you
could write: María, such a soothing *M* . . .
as in manzanilla, your good tea;
as in Michoacán, your good memories.

Remember when I said you were half
of a recipe? When I asked you: how do you know
who you are? unlabeled, unmarked,
like the gravestones of the daughters
you lost two times—once in life

and once in the burial grounds.
I thought that only written words proved
our existence, that only those scribbles with oregano

dots could identify us quicker than
our mothers. But looking at these pictures,

how these unidentified tabloid corpses
can misplace their names—the part
of them foreign to their skins like the stitches
of purple threads—I realize how wrong
I am. Bones are the only columns

keeping us intact. In a photograph,
eyes opened or closed, we are what we've always been
to those who knew us. Abuela, in your pictures,
where the only curves and lines
are wrinkles, there's no mistaking you.

## Slide Transparency of My Now-Deceased Mother Sitting on the Lawn One Day before My Birth

When I hold you to the light I see
through the petals on your glass dress, but not
what's inside the dress itself, which makes me
question whether I was really there.
The bulb's fierce center expanding
in your belly is not evidence enough.

The cuffs and sleeves of the shirts on the line
suspend in the wind at midwave.
You squint, one shoulder
upraised, the way you sit when your back aches.
It is summer, the grape-picking season.
Your mouth half-closed

is narrowing down the syllables of my name.
Half-opened,
it's letting go of what you didn't name me.
You created other paradoxes:
your footfalls fainting as you come closer,
growing stronger as you walk away.

The white wall of the house behind you
is a clear curtain
caught by the camera as it disappears,
unable to expose what breathes inside.

Everything dissolves with hunger.
But let's not talk about the sky peeled off,

about the flesh of your face thinned out.
This is my frame: you
sit translucent and tight-fisted.
I can hold you to the light
or black you out inside my hand.
You cannot escape me.

# Stars Breaking

We've always been violent toward stars.
As children, stick in hand, we strike
at the piñata in the dark, our cousins guide
near-misses with screams, our mothers
suck in their tongues in fear
that we might club the neighbor's son
and knock him to the hospital again
the way one random swing finding his head
did last year. But not even a bleeding ear
or a bandage the color of crushed plums
could stop us from sharpening
the six tasseled corners and raising yet another
star up—that plump belly sacrifice, waiting
for the rib-shattering blow
that throws its contents
out, heavy hearts first. These rewards
are enough to pacify the savages in all of us,
and no skull-cracking or tearing open
of skin as easily as pink tissue-thin paper
can keep the stars from hanging or us
from that inflicted wound and victorious
unhooking. This doesn't keep you up
anymore, Abuelo, bed-ridden, broken-
boned and out-numbered by a riot

of children shrieking like witches on the patio.
Last week you fell off a horse, tonight
that horse goes galloping without you.
Even from that there was a lesson to be learned:
you said we are only mass, becoming
heavier with age, until nothing can endure
the clefts of our wrinkles,
the thickness of our calluses and toes.
Listening to the posada in your sleep,
what, Abuelo, can you make us understand
from that, unafraid to hear a clay
and paper star break open like a peanut
shell between our back teeth? We've
always known those stars are loose
like overcoat buttons, they are elbow scabs,
they're the eye put out by the firecracker, one
of the firecracker's sudden eyes. They're
the glass of the soon-blown fuse,
they're decapitations at the guillotine,
destined long ago to come
tumbling down. Piñata stars teach us
the valuable lesson of defeat,
the lesson of the fall into the dark and how
we each follow that identical path. They show us
not to be disappointed by our loss
of strength or by our separation from
the sky. We are temporary
as these piñata stars, which masquerade
their mortality with three shades of gold
that like the crowns of your two front teeth,
Abuelo, will glitter to the very end,

until that instant when sound overthrows
light, when the blindfold becomes a permanent one,
and the cries become distant as moons . . .
or stars—stars because they float above
you, because you don't need to see them
to know they're no longer a part of what you are.

# Abuelo Photographs

Your mother left you
when you were only ten,
a broken jug, patient
as a flowerpot.
A white man came to take your picture,
you picked up your head
to show you had a neck,
and then you smiled

like the best hypocrite:
mouth split to half grin, eyes
round as the camera lens—
your pretense of comfort
and hard-won fame.
You won first place for pity
and your face froze up that way.
For sixty years

that face has been a sentence for you—
what your mother's absence
molded like ceramic,
the one you thought would bring her back,
if you didn't blink.
Now you're getting weaker,
shrinking back
into that lump of mud you were

before the photograph,
that sad bulk
your mother thought too small to keep,
too dark it might frighten her someday
if she should search her purse
and find you there,
staring up like a humpbacked rat
asking to be fed.

So you took another photograph,
trying to look your best and
as unimposing as a business card,
sharp as a keepsake in Sunday dress.
You hang
in the brightest room,
your eyes nailed open on the wall
wide as the cross of Christ,

looking whiter than you really are
when you interrupt the morning light.
And as you age,
your skins become darker—
the three of you overexposing,
becoming sick of sight.
Your mother wouldn't claim you now
in your charred paper masks, all

burnt cheeks and cooked bone.
Would she recognize any of you,
her Mexican creations, cracked
under the sun like clay?
But should she take her time in coming,
the white man can return

and snap another shot
of you among your photographs:

layered into thin and faded welts,
there will be four of you:
dead quadruplets sharing a single box,
two smiling, two frowning,
all waiting for her hands
to smooth the crinkles out
and rub those gazes off—to love you
for the colored boys you've always been.

# Abuelo Looks at Stars without Glasses

A star is only a smudge
like a dead moth stuck to the window screen, but more
pedestrian—a flake of wing still clinging to the wire
after he leans forward to flick the insect off. Stars

have yet to sharpen hairs, startling
as nettles; have yet to grow hooks like ceiling fixtures.
He squints, calling them
the crusts on a damaged sky, skins thickened inward,

scale-stiff and white—
the fingertipped buds on the lemon tree that prick out
the shadows and threaten to roll the moon off the night.
One night he sees two stars drop,

one chasing after the other,
both breaking off their gowns of light.
With no shell and no bone, he pictures
the body of the second

slowly flattening atop the first,
then igniting like a slug with salt.
There must have been a shriek.
There must have been a closer witness

come across a single sizzling mass.
Either he gave the lump a nudge
or he simply walked past the sound whose slight weight
did not leave a print worthy of notice.

# Ghostory

Their fingers pressed down
on my neck to feel my pulse, to ride
the gush of my blood. They were
the guests
Abuelo said would rise
as soon as I shut the door.

They escaped from his tea-heavy breath
to web the darkest corners.
But their silky muscles were free,
destined to rest somehow
on my shoulders
or in the hollows of my shoes.

Invisible as words, they could be
just as loud, taking over my room,
making me its only prisoner
the way a tin cup makes a hostage of its coin:
all sides at one time,
especially when the occupant moves.

Afraid to relax an arm under the sheets,
I suppressed a twitch for fear the mattress springs
would call them to my side.
Only my nose poked out.
My comfort was, that like Abuelo,
I could always breathe them out.

But Abuelo continued to produce them.
He'd let them crack their sounds
each time he yawned.
He slept in the bed next to mine.
I could hear them sneaking off until one night
he emptied his mouth of them completely.

Years later,
I'm learning to live with them.
They are part of me, part of my night.
They wrap around my skin
like the cloud of translucent winds
that envelops the full moon's curves.

They've wedged their limbs
into the lines of my face, its reflection.
They've taken over my shadow
and are molding it to fit their needs.
Soon, I'll have a rounded back like Abuelo;
my head will tilt forward with their weight.

My body belongs to them.
They have found their place inside me.
I let them go, then call them back, softly.
I send out my voice to seek out *my* grandchildren.
They will keep me talking
when I can no longer speak for myself.

# What Smells Dead

If through whisper and caress we sense them,
if the yellow light sneaking out
at the splitting of their bones betrays them,
why not notice the dead through smell?

Grandfathers, those smokers,
are subtle, dismissing an aroma of breath
penetrated by the lit match
or of that final suck—the faint burning up
of the filter's edge
as if in quiet protest for having been buried

in clean coats. Old women take
their old women smells and insist
on keeping them clasped
to their clothes like spare bobby pins;
but their graves will radiate like warm glass,
the air made heavy—
the odor of burnt sugar escaping the pot.

The dead don't always have idle smells,
like those that linger at the tips
of gloves or those that rise from the mouths of shoes,
from the chair just emptied;

there is also the discharge of passions.
In lovers, the older the corpse, the stronger the letting go.
Secrets finally resurface,

the skin submits to its own decay.
Hands set free their collection of sticky oils;
necks and thighs give up the touch
in other hands, the scent of money;
tongues release their love of liquor, of tongues.

The rest are also gluttons; they smell of basil
and clove. Their bodies exhume the spices
that in death consume the flesh.

Yet frequently the dead remain unnoticed—
we believe they no longer smell like us.
At night, these smells don't wake us,
but we still absorb them, then breathe them out.
Through us
they settle on the moss like sweat.

# Growing Up with Goya's *Saturno*

In Michoacán he wasn't called Saturno,
nor was he a painting, vulnerable
as the hand that stroked his hair and kept him wild-
eyed as if shocked by his swallowing up of his own
child—perhaps an act he had only fantasized about
but which he had now been forced to commit.

He wasn't confined to the page of an elementary textbook;
he could easily let go the body like a candle
from his grasp and unfold his leg, stepping
down in the dark with a heavy but undetectable
foot. In my world he could blink,
his lashes struck like hatchet marks against his cheeks

as he followed my scent to the bed.
Once there he'd pull back the hair from his ears,
listened for the guilty breathing of a boy
who had not yet coated his tongue with a Credo
or at least three Ave Marías. He did not yet have a name,
but he took up so much space searching

for the smell of my curious fingers, which I had
burdened with my most forbidden openings and which I thought
too heavy to bear the sign of the cross. I'd stay up
wondering how I'd unstick my limbs from the walls
inside his belly once he'd swallowed me up; how I'd keep myself
apart from that confusion of tides and contractions—

from the dirty linens in a room so private, no
guardian angel had yet gone in to explain away the shadows.
He became an anticipation then. He became a Sunday fever,
an excuse from evening Mass. His were the sounds
of beds too passionate to be discreet. His was the light switch
blacked out and made to reappear in some distant house.

He became the collector of the oppressed tongue, that scholar
kept quiet beneath the Eucharist. So when this convocation
claimed its name outside of Michoacán, away from México—
*Saturno*—it quietly stepped back onto the page, its bones rigid
as print, but with its mouth propped open as if at any moment
it could change its mind—complete what I had once begun.

# Sinister Hand

"The left hand," said the Catholic sage, "is the criminal's
hand." And we believed him, granting the right hand
the right to form the cross of Christ against the face,
the right to monopolize the fork, the right to define
all indentations on the body, furrowing paths
down to the feet without committing sin; the right
to keep things proper. The criminal's hand, continued the sage,
would have left us godless; the criminal's hand
would have let us starve; it would have never gone beyond

the crotch. And so my father explained why he burnt me
with the soup spoon. I had used my left hand, the criminal's
hand, to stir the soup. I had brought it up too close
to my mouth—I might have tasted its salts, addicted
my tongue. It came too close to my nose—I might have been
tempted to seek out more private smells.
Such tricky fingers, trying to delve their way inside
like worms to poke and itch until they take command.
And I, careless boy, wanting to stick that hand in my mouth

to lick it clean of all its bitterness, its sharp guilt.
My father burnt me again the next morning, convinced
that the bones on my left hand were reaching out to deviancy,
destined to long for a wallet on a bus, a purse on a park bench,
or, even worse, a knife carefully concealed,
eager and fast like a sixth left finger. Who knows
what else my father thought capable of my left hand,

as it followed me to the bath, as it waited next to me in bed,
deceptive in its patience for the blankets to come down.

I'm still using my left hand to bathe, I would tell my father,
I no longer trust the sage, his once-wise words.
Yet I still remember the lessons with the soup spoon
and how they rolled up my left hand into a fist—
a wounded pet seeking its comfort
against my chest, in the warmth between my legs, and sometimes
under the flesh of the right hand—the forgiving hand—
my father's hand, God's hand, the hand with enough strength
to lift a soup spoon, with enough fury to strike.

# Texaco Alex

Biting into the telephone, brother,
is what I do best when you put me on hold
and I sit with a hollow receiver,
trying to make the half-spoken word last
like a spoonful of ice cream on the tongue.

With you on the line
I know how to surprise my face with its mouth open.
I know thoughts drop hands on the lap
like I know my shoes point to the door
and won't step out.

I called not to say, not to punctuate a sentence,
not to fatten up the wire with buzz.
Remember me? I'm the kid who ate the soggy tomatoes
off your fideo, the one who carried those numbers
to the left on the mathematics page. And here I am now,

completing responses for you in my head:
you're okay, you're off on Wednesday,
the rich wouldn't pump their own lungs.
You miss me. Admit it,
you want to keep me from hanging up

and that's why I'm here, polite with breath
ready to be your company when you please.
A music box works that way:

lift the cover to hear the old tune play.
I know about reliability. Monday nights at eleven

I dial the Texaco station.
I count on hearing the register bleep,
on picking up a customer's change, on you
handing me a dead receiver—
a dry nozzle waiting to have the pump switched on.

# Taking Possession

I'll begin with the simple things:
your extra comb, your sock, learning to trace
a strand of brown hair until I darken it,
exhaust it between my fingers;
learning to fill in the shape of your foot

with my fist. I'll do this every night for a week.
When I'm ready, I'll slide the comb back onto the crowded dresser
and replace the sock where you last left it,
taking up the space behind the hamper. Then I'll claim
the indigo button on your favorite purple shirt and the bookmark

keeping page 130 from
131. These I will not return as quickly, not until
I master slipping the button on my tongue,
trapping it against the roof of my mouth like candy,
which can never surrender its sugar. But it's not a flavor

I crave, but the image of your shirt, opened
at the sternum, exposing that dividing line, which ends
on your upper belly. Perhaps you'll never wear
that shirt again. Perhaps it will hang in the closet,
completely unbuttoned. Then it will all be mine.

The bookmark I'll remove to make you lose
your place in *Cien años de soledad,*

though when you find page 130, 131
will be missing. I'll finish it for you, out loud.
I'll stand before the mirror, imitating the tones

you make when you say, "Tú," when you utter,
"Sí." And once I too own the gift of shrinking
the lips into a knot, enclosing them to a perfect *o,*
we can read the rest of that page together: you
mouthing the syllable, me reflecting it. I'll practice

breathing out the way you do when you write
and when you sleep, a sound so slight, so soothing
it must not have come from the nose, but from a stranger
source. I'll mimic this strangeness until not even I
can detect my listening.

And while you're gone, threatening never to return,
I'll learn from your soap
how to conform my hands and feet to the nooks
on your body; from the pillow, I'll lift the creases
the right side of your neck has left behind.

Your couch will teach me all about positions;
the light switch will coach me on the craft of unbending
angles into lines. And when I learn to open the door
the way you do, knowing exactly what you find,
I'll enter, burdening the carpet with your weight,

smelling of afternoon sweat, damp cotton, and glazed skin—
brown like yours. I'll fool this chair, this bed,
and especially these walls when I approach them
with your heat. I'll keep your possessions
perceptive, greeting you through me.

# So Often the Pitcher Goes to Water until It Breaks

(a poem in four voices)

**1.**

You know what they say, manita,
so often the pitcher goes to water,
so often the man reaches in
to tickle, to probe, to run his finger
across your leg the way the designs
move slowly around the water pitcher, disappearing
long enough to tease and coming back in time
to find their place so smoothly
that your eye fills in the gaps.
And as night leaks into day,
this man will wash his hand
in the lake before going home, thinking his wife
will never trace those dirty fingernails
to the oils in your sweat.
And what will you have then?
A thumbprint etched against your thigh
as visible as a smear on the pitcher's clay.

**2.**

It's not because of his longest fingers,
not their crawling out, searching for an itch,
not their settling on the knee, docile
and moist as a dog's nose. It's not because of his knuckle
or its five hard nipples. And it's not his wrist,

that cool tongue. Those arms, smooth thighs, are not
why I let him submerge his body into mine.
It's his resurfacing, when he
closes his arms, tucks in his wrist, covers
his knuckles, withdraws his fingers,
taking part of me with him the way the pitcher
takes away its drink from the lake—discreet enough
to make the villagers think it is still intact.
It's when he emerges and goes home with me in his belly
that I learn to occupy his salts.
Those hollow bodyprints he left behind? I'm
filling them up with myself, making myself
expand. I am

        stretching. I am

                getting larger.
Soon I will be all oceans, deep stomachs,
and when I swallow him next, I won't want to spit him back.


3.

The secret is in their curves, compadre, women
are all roundness—hips, buttocks, breasts,
elbows, ankles, shoulderblades—it's all
in the way you collect them, how you
take each ring and slide it on your finger,
how you begin with the smallest circle
and make it the heart of a bigger one, which in turn
is the heart a bigger one, just like the ripples
in the lake, with so many centers that no matter which
you pull out of the water, it is absolutely the heart
of something. Of course, compadre, you cannot call them
circles, or rings, and it would not be wise to tell them
that there are so many of them. Tell her

she is one. Tell her she is the reflection of the moon,
but don't tell her that means there are two
of them then, and that she is the second one,
or that the moon has her own reflection at the lake
already, or that anyone can take
that reflection home in their water pitcher,
or that anyone can drink the moon that night
and expel it by the following morning.
Don't tell her, compadre, that even the moon
has curves, and that those curves, like any other
curves, can possess a touch or a look
but can never control the hand or own the eye.

4.

Only so much will I pretend this rete-cabrón
kept his hands in his pockets all day, fingers
folded down like a puppy's ears.
Only so much will I believe he kept his prick
tail-limp and tame between his thighs, thighs
so weak, they're as quick to spread apart
as a mouth opening long before the tongue wants out.
I don't need to sniff his hands
to know they've been digging up
new smells; I don't need to touch his feet
to know the toes have been dipped in a stranger's
sheets. It's all in the way he walks in
through the door—tilted, half-tipped
like a pitcher, having just given itself
out. He thinks there's plenty of himself to pour,
poor thing. Soon he'll have emptied out
completely, and he'll be easier to crack,
weightless shell. And how much

of himself will he carry then? What part of him
won't leak out and sink through the floor?
You know what they say:
So often the pitcher goes to water—
Tanto va el cántaro al agua—
So often the pitcher goes to water
until it breaks.

# The Man Who Gives You Nightmares

He's an agnostic—keep your crosses
down, hang up your rosaries.
Nothing holds his visits back:

not the latches on your doors,
not the saints above your bed.
He doesn't smell the garlic.

He can pierce a wall much quicker
than the shrill you gave
the time you thought you saw him.

But he's much, much more discreet,
slowly creeping in: one foot
stirring up the dust,

the other settling that dust.
And his hands hold up his frock
like a bulk of shadows,

which he spreads across your bed
to keep your limbs at rest
while he unfolds his bones

like pocketknives. His heart
slumps over on his fence of ribs
like an opened mailbag—

it's where he keeps bad dreams.
He reaches in and plucks one drop
of blood and tucks it

carefully inside your ear.
It slides down like a sinker;
it tickles like a hook.

But there's no waking up—
there is no light switch near enough
to coat the dark.

Tonight you hear the stuttering
of wings. You climb the alamo,
release the pair of swallows

from their trap of twigs.
But before they shrink into the sky,
their bodies turn to stones.

And you stand underneath
looking up, just waiting
for the first to fall.

One's coming down, beak first
and pointing at your eye.
The tip is coming closer,

and closer, and closer . . .
The spirit's job is done.
When you awake, dizzy

in a room of spinning shadows,
you think you see him once again,
and once again you scream.

But don't be scared.
He'll leave depressions on your sheets,
damp as body stains.

He'll leave dry chips of soil
on the floor like broken glass.
He might even leave a bruise.

But he leaves.
He always leaves. By dawn,
yes, he's absolutely gone.

## Illinois Poetry Series

*Laurence Lieberman, Editor*

Floating on Solitude
*Dave Smith* (3-volume reissue, 1996)

Bruised Paradise
*Kevin Stein* (1996)

Walt Whitman Bathing
*David Wagoner* (1996)

Rough Cut
*Thomas Swiss* (1997)

Paris
*Jim Barnes* (1997)

The Ways We Touch
*Miller Williams* (1997)

The Rooster Mask
*Henry Hart* (1998)

The Trouble-Making Finch
*Len Roberts* (1998)

Grazing
*Ira Sadoff* (1998)

Turn Thanks
*Lorna Goodison* (1999)

Traveling Light: Collected and New
   Poems
*David Wagoner* (1999)

Some Jazz a While: Collected Poems
*Miller Williams* (1999)

## National Poetry Series

Eroding Witness
*Nathaniel Mackey* (1985)
Selected by Michael S. Harper

Palladium
*Alice Fulton* (1986)
Selected by Mark Strand

Cities in Motion
*Sylvia Moss* (1987)
Selected by Derek Walcott

The Hand of God and a Few
Bright Flowers
*William Olsen* (1988)
Selected by David Wagoner

The Great Bird of Love
*Paul Zimmer* (1989)
Selected by William Stafford

Stubborn
*Roland Flint* (1990)
Selected by Dave Smith

The Surface
*Laura Mullen* (1991)
Selected by C. K. Williams

The Dig
*Lynn Emanuel* (1992)
Selected by Gerald Stern

My Alexandria
*Mark Doty* (1993)
Selected by Philip Levine

The High Road to Taos
*Martin Edmunds* (1994)
Selected by Donald Hall

Theater of Animals
*Samn Stockwell* (1995)
Selected by Louise Glück

The Broken World
*Marcus Cafagña* (1996)
Selected by Yusef Komunyakaa

Nine Skies
*A. V. Christie* (1997)
Selected by Sandra McPherson

Lost Wax
*Heather Ramsdell* (1998)
Selected by James Tate

So Often the Pitcher Goes to Water
   until It Breaks
*Rigoberto González* (1999)
Selected by Ai

## Other Poetry Volumes

*Local Men* and *Domains*
*James Whitehead* (1987)

Her Soul beneath the Bone: Women's
   Poetry on Breast Cancer
*Edited by Leatrice Lifshitz* (1988)

Days from a Dream Almanac
*Dennis Tedlock* (1990)

Working Classics: Poems on Industrial
   Life
*Edited by Peter Oresick and Nicholas Coles*
   (1990)

Hummers, Knucklers, and Slow
   Curves: Contemporary Baseball
   Poems
*Edited by Don Johnson* (1991)

The Double Reckoning of Christopher
   Columbus
*Barbara Helfgott Hyett* (1992)

Selected Poems
*Jean Garrigue* (1992)

New and Selected Poems, 1962-92
*Laurence Lieberman* (1993)

*The Dig* and *Hotel Fiesta*
*Lynn Emanuel* (1994)

For a Living: The Poetry of Work
*Edited by Nicholas Coles and Peter Oresick*
   (1995)

The Tracks We Leave: Poems on
   Endangered Wildlife of North
   America
*Barbara Helfgott Hyett* (1996)

Peasants Wake for Fellini's *Casanova*
   and Other Poems
*Andrea Zanzotto; edited and translated by*
   *John P. Welle and Ruth Feldman; draw-*
   *ings by Federico Fellini and Augusto*
   *Murer* (1997)

*Moon in a Mason Jar* and *What My Father*
   *Believed*
*Robert Wrigley* (1997)

The Wild Card: Selected Poems, Early
   and Late
*Karl Shapiro; edited by Stanley Kunitz and*
   *David Ignatow* (1998)

Typeset in 10/14 Cycles
with Cycles display
Designed by Dennis Roberts
Composed by Jim Proefrock
at the University of Illinois Press
Manufactured by Cushing-Malloy, Inc.

University of Illinois Press
1325 South Oak Street
Champaign, IL 61820-6903
www.press.uillinois.edu